spain

by

DR. GEORGE KISH

University of Michigan

ANN ARBOR, MICHIGAN

NELSON DOUBLEDAY, INC.   GARDEN CITY, N.Y.

*Prepared with the cooperation of the
American Geographical Society*

The flag of Spain, once the symbol of an empire upon which the sun never set, is still the emblem of a proud nation.

THE FLAG OF SPAIN was the first flag of a European nation to fly over the Americas. The patrons of Columbus were Ferdinand and Isabella of Spain, and for centuries the destinies of Spain and of a good part of the Americas were one. Though Spain no longer rules any part of the Western Hemisphere, its speech, its art, its political and social traditions have been preserved everywhere south of the Rio Grande, except in Brazil.

Four hundred years ago Spain ruled an empire over which the sun never set. The great galleons sailing to Spanish ports brought with them gold and silver and precious stones, the wealth of two hemispheres. Spain then was the first power in Europe and in the world.

Land of Two Seas

SPAIN occupies most of the Iberian Peninsula whose shores are washed by the Atlantic Ocean on the north and west, and by the Mediter-

3

ranean Sea on the south and east. It was destined to be a sea power, and much of its history has been that of expansion across the bordering seas, to Italy, to Africa, and to the Americas. Its mark was left on all these lands, where Spanish styles of architecture, Spanish words, and Spanish customs survived long after the forces of Spain had withdrawn.

Spanish history begins at the dawn of European civilization. In the north a range of high, rugged mountains separates the central tableland, or *meseta,* from the small coves and valleys of the Atlantic coast. Caves discovered in these mountains contain wall paintings that are among the earliest known European works of art. There, prehistoric man sketched scenes of great beauty and striking color, figures of hunters stalking buffalo and deer, that in their simplicity and strength still impress the visitor. These drawings in caves like Altamira mark the beginnings of civilization on Spanish soil. But written history begins much later, when one of the earliest seafaring nations of the Old World, the Phoenicians, landed on the south and east coasts of Spain.

Merchants of Copper and Purple Cloth

MORE THAN a thousand years before Christ, the Phoenicians established trading posts on the coasts of Spain, where they bartered purple cloth and jewelry against native copper and grain. The earliest Spanish cities, Cádiz and Málaga in the south, were founded by Phoenician merchants.

Hispania: Roman Spain

ABOUT 200 B.C., Spain became Rome's first overseas colony. Hispania, the name given to the peninsula by the Romans, is the origin of the word "Spain" in all European languages. Spain remained part of the Roman empire for 600 years, and those centuries left an indelible mark on the country.

The roads Rome built served Spain until modern times. In some parts

16.   AQUEDUCT, SEGOVIA

The great aqueduct of Segovia was built by the Roman Emperor Augustus, of great blocks of granite, held together without either mortar or clamps. For nearly 2,000 years, it has supplied the city with water from the nearby hills.

5

of the country off the beaten track it is still possible to find a stretch of Roman pavement, its great flagstones marked by the wheels of Roman chariots, or to cross a handsomely arched bridge that has carried traffic now for 2,000 years. The magnificent Roman aqueduct at Segovia, built during the lifetime of Christ, continues to bring water to the town, and the high arches of the aqueduct shelter people from the midday sun as they have done for centuries.

Above all, Roman rule gave Spain two of its most precious possessions, its language and its religion. Spanish is directly descended from Latin, the speech of Rome. It is the language that Spanish conquest spread from the Philippines to Peru, from California to Chile. Spain embraced Christianity at an early date, and its steadfast support of the Catholic faith earned its rulers the title of "Catholic Kings."

Vandals and Goths, the Blonds of Spain

STARTING ABOUT A.D. 300, the Roman empire slowly disintegrated under the blows of the barbarians from the north. Spain was invaded and conquered in the fifth century by the Vandals, a German tribe whose raids made their name a word of terror throughout the empire. The Vandals, in turn, were driven from Spain by another Germanic tribe, the Goths, who then ruled Spain for two centuries. Blond and blue-eyed, the Goths brought a new element into the crucible where the Spanish people were being formed. A thousand years later

the Aztecs of Mexico and the Incas of Peru were to gape in awe at the blond giants who came ashore in the first waves of Spanish conquest.

Eight Centuries of Islam

THE RULE of the Goths in Spain was brought to an end by the surging strength of Islam, the religion founded by the prophet Mohammed, whose followers are known as Moslems. It was a fighting, conquering religion, bent upon extending its creed to a large part of the world, and it quickly rallied the superb fighters of the Arab tribes. Within fifty years of Mohammed's death, by 682, Islam had conquered all of the Near East, Arabia, Persia, Egypt, and by 710 the green flag of Mohammed was raised all over North Africa. In 711 the first Moslem forces crossed the Strait of Gibraltar from North Africa into Spain.

The name of this strait, and of the great rock that towers above it, forming a natural fortress, is a memorial to the general who led the forces of Islam to Spain, Tarik. *Gebel-al-Tarik*, the rock of Tarik, became Gibraltar, one of the hundreds of Arabic names that the Moslems left behind as part of their legacy to Spain. Within five years of the first landings the last remnants of the Christian forces escaped into the mountains of the far north. For nearly eight centuries, a foreign religion, Islam, ruled much of Spain, and the traveler encounters the works of that time in many places.

But resistance to this alien element began very early. The long fight to drive the Moslems from the country looms large in the annals of Spain. It served as the anvil on which Spanish unity was forged, as the uniting bond between the various Christian kingdoms and principalities that arose as the "reconquest" progressed. In the end, it was the final victory over the Moslems, in 1492, that ushered in the new era of a united Spain.

Moslem Art

THE EIGHT CENTURIES of Moslem influence in Spain were not all spent in war. There was the existence, side by side, of Christian,

The Gate of the Sun stands guard over the entrance to Toledo. It is one of the best examples of the art of Moorish craftsmen, with its horseshoe arch, and turreted battlements.

25.   "GATE OF THE SUN," TOLEDO

Moslem, and Jew, the mingling of West and East, that created works of art and bequeathed a scientific tradition that is one of the glories of Spain. There was tolerance for the various religions, too, described in such words as *Mozárabe,* a Christian living under Moslem kings, and *Mudejar,* a Moslem living in Christian territory. Cities like Toledo, Seville, Córdoba, and Granada are treasure houses of these times, when Spain was the most prosperous, the most civilized part of Europe.

Arab architects brought the horseshoe arch to Spain, and such monuments as the Puerta del Sol, the Sun Gate of Toledo, have preserved it to our time. Moslem places of worship, like the Great Mosque of Córdoba, with its hundreds of columns, each of exquisite workmanship, each of different material, each of different shape, are still standing, saved because they were transformed into Christian churches. The Giralda of Seville, the great tower of Seville Cathedral, that stands above the city and the fertile plain that surrounds it, was originally the tower of a mosque, whence the priest called the faithful to prayer. Its chiseled, lacelike decorations are among the best works of Arabic stone masonry.

Granada, Gem of Moslem Art in Spain

G RANADA, of all Spanish cities, is the place where the exquisite detail of Moslem architecture, the perfect balance of archway and court, reached its highest level. Granada was the last refuge of Moslem rulers when the rest of Spain had returned to Christian control. There the palace of the Alhambra was built, high on a hill, against the white

The Giralda is the bell tower and principal landmark of Seville. It was built in the twelfth century as a minaret, or prayer tower, by the Moorish kings. The statue on its peak stands some 300 feet above the city.

10.   THE GIRALDA, SEVILLE

9

background of the snowy peaks of the Sierra Nevada, where patio and fountain, balcony and staircase display the genius of Arab builders. A short distance from the Alhambra hill stand the gardens of the Generalife, another legacy of Islam to Spain, the art of using trees, flowers, fountains, and flowing water to create a man-made landscape of exquisite beauty.

At the foot of the hills spreads the fertile plain, the *vega*, of Granada. Islam brought the art of irrigation to Spain, the skill to capture water and bring it to thirsty fields, distributing it through an

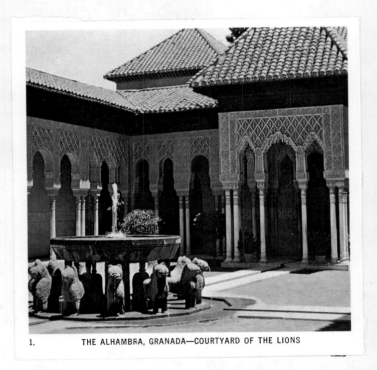

1.   THE ALHAMBRA, GRANADA—COURTYARD OF THE LIONS

The art of Moslem Spain reached its highest level in the Alhambra, the palace of the Moorish kings of Granada. There, amidst fountains and gardens, the Moslem craftsmen created masterpieces of marble, tile, and mosaics, sunny courtyards, and shaded halls.

View of the beautiful gardens of the Alhambra, the Moorish palace-fortress in Granada. The *Torre de las Damas* shown here is part of the women's quarters.

Granada, one of Spain's most colorful cities, is perched high above the fertile valley named after it. In the steep, narrow streets one often catches a glimpse of the green fields below.

intricate system of weirs and canals, and thus creating prosperous farms in an otherwise dry country. Besides irrigation, the period of Moslem rule in Spain also saw the introduction of new crops, fruits, sugar, rice, and cotton, from the East. The names of some of the new crops, too, were taken over from the Arabic, and like the names of mountains, rivers, and towns, remain in the Spanish language to this day. *Alcalde,* the judge; *almirante,* the ruler of the fleet; these are among the hundreds of Arabic words adapted by the Spaniards, some of which were to find their way into other European languages as well.

Painted, glazed tiles like these, called *azulejo*, have been made since the days of Moslem rule; their colors are an ornament to houses and courtyards all over Spain.

Córdoban Leather and Toledo Steel

WHEN the Moslems came to Spain, the civilization of the Christian West had not yet recovered from the blows of the centuries-long barbarian invasions. Moslem craftsmen were far superior to any Europeans then. Toledo swords were the best of medieval Europe, and the tradition of ornate metalwork is kept alive in the city today. The old English word for leatherworker, "cordwainer," harks back to the days when Córdoba made the best leather goods of Europe; the elaborately carved wooden grilles that stand in front of the altar in many a Spanish church are the work of craftsmen schooled in the traditions of Moslem as well as Christian Spain.

The role of Spain as an intermediary between the Christian world and the world of Islam was of the greatest importance in the development of European learning and literature. Much of what we possess of the works of Greek and Roman philosophy, literature, and science was saved through its translation into Arabic in the early Middle Ages. This classical heritage was then brought by Moslem and Jewish scholars to Spain, where they met and mingled with Christian scholars from all over Europe. Toledo and other Spanish cities were among the greatest centers of European learning a thousand years ago; here the knowledge of Greece and Rome, and the skills of the Moslems in medicine, astronomy, and mathematics, were translated from Arabic into Latin, and thus were brought back to the intellectual world of Europe.

Castile, León, and Aragón: the Cradle of Spain

DURING THE CENTURIES of struggle between Christian and Moslem Spain the elements of the country as we know them today slowly came into being. The heart of the peninsula, the high, dry tableland, was the birthplace of the kingdom of Castile and León, whose flag Columbus carried to the New World. The valley of the Ebro River, in the northeast, saw the rise of the kingdom of Aragón, and it was the marriage of Ferdinand of Aragón to Isabella of Castile that united Spain.

In the far northeast, separated from France by the high mountain wall of the Pyrenees, Barcelona, ancestor of Catalonia, developed a merchant realm, where the seafaring tradition of Spain was born. In the southwest, Andalusia, one of the last regions of Spain to be given up by Islam, became the grain chamber of the country, and its port, Seville, was to be Spain's principal gateway to the New World.

Columbus Sails for the West

THE FALL OF GRANADA, in 1492, ushers in the new era of a united and powerful Spain. Conquest of this last Moslem stronghold on Spanish soil was an event celebrated all over the Christian world. This military success, and the desire to outdo little Portugal in finding a seaway to the wealth of the Indies, gave Columbus the support of Spain.

Palos is a small, sleepy port on the southwestern coast. There the three tiny ships of Columbus hoisted their sails in the summer of 1492,

This letter written by Columbus, is found, together with many other famous documents of the Age of Discovery, in the Archives of the Indies, in Seville.

and disappeared into the west, to search for a new route to the Indies. When Columbus sailed from Palos, he was an aging man, driven by his deep conviction that a seaway to India could be found, a conviction scarcely shared by anyone else. When he and his men returned in 1493, he was feted throughout the country as a hero. As his monument in Seville Cathedral proclaims: Columbus gave a new world to Castile and León!

In one of the courtyards surrounding the cathedral, the patio of the orange trees, stands a little building where the remnants of Columbus' library are preserved, including the cosmographies, descriptions of the universe, with Columbus' handwritten notes.

Seville: Treasure House of the Indies

NEXT DOOR to the Seville Cathedral are the Archives of the Indies, in a building called the House of Commerce, that was the nerve

11.   TOWER OF GOLD, SEVILLE

The Golden Tower of Seville was one of the towers of the Alcázar, the fortified castle of the Moorish rulers of Spain built mainly in the 1300's. Galleons carrying the treasure of the Indies often anchored in the shadow of the Golden Tower.

center of Spanish-American relations. The Archives of the Indies display documents of the three centuries of Spanish rule over the Americas: the treaty of 1494, whereby Spain and Portugal divided the world between them, the maps and pilot books of Spanish discoverers, the reports of Viceroys from Mexico and Peru and Chile. The Spanish galleons landed gold and silver, lead and copper, cotton, sugar, and molasses on the quays of Seville, and Spain during that golden age was the richest, most powerful nation of Europe.

Spain, a World Empire

THE GRANDSON and great-grandson of Ferdinand and Isabella, Charles I and Philip II, were the kings under whom Spain had its greatest glory. In the affairs of Europe its word was decisive, in the world beyond the Atlantic its rule was uncontested from the Philippines to the West Indies. This, too, was the Golden Age of Spanish arts and

MADRID

BURGOS

BERNABEU STADIUM
Ave. de Gen. Perón

METROPOLITAN STADIUM

UNIVERSITY CITY

NEW MINISTRIES

MUSEUM OF NATURAL SCIENCE

ZARAGOZA & BARCELONA

Ave. de la America

EL ESCORIAL

Paseo de la Moncloa

SOROLLA MUSEUM

PARQUE DEL OESTE

ARCH OF TRIUMPH

MINISTRY OF AIR

Paseo de Pintor Rosales

Paseo de la Castellana

PLAZA DE TOROS (Bullring)

Alcala

BARAJAS AIRPORT

PANTHEON OF GOYA

COLUMBUS MONUMENT

C. de Goya

Plaza de España

CERVANTES MONUMENT

PALACE OF JUSTICE

NAT'L LIBRARY & MUSEUM

Calle de

CASA DE CAMPO

NORTH STATION

WAR OFFICE

PUERTA DE ALCALA

ROYAL OPERA

ROYAL ACADEMY OF FINE ARTS

Plaza de Cibeles

Plaza de la Independencia

ROYAL PALACE

PANADERIA

Puerta del Sol

FOUNTAIN OF NEPTUNE

ROYAL ACADEMY

JARDINES DEL RETIRO

ZOOLOGICAL GARDENS

CATHEDRAL

Calle Mayor

NIÑO JESUS STATION

GOYA STA.

Calle de Segovia

Plaza Mayor

Calle de Atocha

PRADO MUSEUM

BOTANICAL GARDENS

CHURCH OF SAN FRANCISCO

EL RASTRO (Market)

Calle de Toledo

OBSERVATORY

IMPERIAL STA.

ATOCHA STATION

VALENCIA

Rio

Ave. de la Ciudad de Barcelona

LAS PEÑUELAS STA.

LAS DELICIAS STATION

Manzanares

TOLEDO

CADIZ

letters. Between 1500 and 1700 lived the greatest writers and painters and architects to appear on the Spanish scene. The epic of overseas conquest was described by the historians of the heroic age, by Oviedo and by Bishop Las Casas, the first defender of the human rights of the Indians. Lope de Vega and Calderón re-created in their many plays the figures of Spanish life at court and in the villages, and they are counted among the founders of modern drama.

Don Quijote, "Knight of the Sad Countenance"

GREATEST OF ALL Spanish writers was Miguel Cervantes, a soldier who lost an arm in the wars against the Turks, and turned poet and novelist. He created one of the immortal figures of fiction, the Knight of the Sad Countenance, Don Quijote. "Don Quijote" is one of the masterpieces of Spanish literature, an enormous canvas of the Spain of Cervantes' time, a picture of customs and morals, a political and literary satire. The tall, thin knight, defender of high ideals, impractical but loyal to the last, and the short, portly Sancho Panza, his shrewd, down-to-earth companion, ride through the rolling landscape, through adventures comic and tragic in turn. And it is truly easy to imagine the

The statue of Don Quijote, the "Knight of the Sad Countenance," and of his faithful, tubby companion, Sancho Panza, brings to life two of the world's most famous figures of fiction.

19.   STATUE OF DON QUIJOTE, MADRID

21.　　　　MONASTERY OF EL ESCORIAL, NEAR MADRID

On the slopes of mountains near Madrid, Philip II built this monastery to the glory of God, and as a monument to his royal house. It
is one of the masterpieces of Spanish art.

lone figure of Don Quijote, astride his lean old horse, tilting against
the windmills in single combat, when one sees windmills that still turn
their tall, canvas-covered wings above the dry stubble of La Mancha,
Don Quijote's country.

Escorial: a Royal Tomb

THE PATRONAGE of kings, nobles, and clergy, suddenly enriched by
the flow of wealth from the Americas, endowed Spain with
churches, palaces, and monasteries that proclaim the ideals of the
Golden Age. The most striking of these, and the most singular in pur-
pose is the Escorial, royal palace, great tomb, monastery, that stands
in the hills near Madrid. Philip II built the Escorial as his country
residence, and as a monument to himself and to his royal house. In its
burial vault lie all the Spanish monarchs, the kings on the right, their
queens on the left. The magnificent symmetry of the palace built on
the pattern of a gridiron, the tapestries and paintings inside, the marble

El Greco, one of the great painters of Spain's Golden Age, lived for many years in this pleasant and simple house, with its tiny garden, on a side street in Toledo.

14.   EL GRECO'S HOUSE, TOLEDO

and gold and precious stones of the church, the rare books and manuscripts of the library make it one of the masterpieces of Spanish art and architecture.

Called "The Greek," El Greco Was
One of Spain's Greatest Painters

THE SPANIARDS of the Golden Age could call on the best artists of the time to decorate their dwellings and churches. El Greco, a Greek by birth, was the first of the great Spanish painters, who spent most of his mature years in Toledo. That city is the setting for some of his best-known canvases, where he reproduced with superb artistry the somber colors of the landscape, the intensely religious faces of priests, the haughty and handsome nobles of his time.

Ribera, Velásquez, and Murillo were the leading figures of the period following that of El Greco. To these great artists we owe masterful portraits of kings and young princes, vivid likenesses of the common people, and moving paintings of religious significance, many of them now in one of the world's most famous art galleries, the Prado of Madrid. Victoria, contemporary of El Greco, composed some of the greatest works of church music of all time, and he is considered to be one of the creators of modern musical forms.

Loyola, Founder of the Jesuits

S PAIN has always been a strong Catholic country, where religious fervor found ready expression in the fighting spirit of the long wars against Islam. When the supremacy of the Catholic Church was challenged by the Reformation in the sixteenth century, Spain was in the forefront of the religious wars. One of the leaders of the fight between the Catholic and Protestant churches was Ignatius de Loyola, a Spaniard. Ex-soldier, like Cervantes, wounded in war like his contemporary, Loyola became the founder of the Society of Jesus, the Jesuit order. The Jesuits were organized like a militant order from the first, and they have carried the word of the Church, as missionaries and teachers, to the far corners of the earth. The history of the Americas is closely connected with the explorations of Jesuit missionaries, such as Father Marquette, in the

The pomp and pageantry of the Spanish Church is seen at its best during the great processions of Holy Week, when religious societies parade in their traditional and colorful garb.

9. HOLY WEEK PROCESSION, CUENCA

Great Lakes region, and Father Kino, who established the missions of Arizona.

The participation of Spain in the wars of sixteenth-century Europe meant an enormous sacrifice to the country. This was particularly serious since Spain was colonizing the Americas at the same time, and sent some of its best sons to Mexico and Chile, Peru and Argentina, while other Spaniards were fighting on battlefields all over Europe. Not all the gold of the Americas could support the ambitious schemes of the Spanish kings: and when the greatest fleet of warships ever seen, the great Armada, sailed against England in 1588, it was utterly destroyed.

Years of Decline

SPAIN'S STRENGTH, sapped by expensive wars, lacking the support of vigorous trade and industry, began to ebb towards the end of the sixteenth century. Yet Spanish rule in the Americas remained for another 200 years, and Spain continued to be a power to be reckoned with until almost 1800. Nearly every Spanish city and town has some fine monument to show that if there was a decline, it was slow and gradual. The colonies, it is true, no longer sent back the same flow of wealth as during the Golden Age, but overseas, at least, Spanish rule remained unchallenged until after the American Revolution.

The Independence of the Spanish Americas

THE EVENTS that led to the independence of the United States had a profound influence on the Spanish dominions in the New World. In the early 1800's Spain was invaded and occupied by the troops of Napoleon, and the government was no longer able to control the revolutionary flame that spread across the Spanish Americas. By the end of the 1820's the republics south of the Rio Grande came into being, and Spain only retained control over Puerto Rico and Cuba in the Americas, and over the Philippines in the Far East.

The nineteenth century was a difficult time for Spain, racked by civil wars, and seriously hit by the loss of most of its colonial empire. There was progress in the economic field, though, brought about by the building of railroads and the development of new industries, especially in the north, where iron and steel plants came into being, and around Barcelona in the east.

"Remember the Maine!"

THE SPANISH-AMERICAN war in 1898 meant the loss of nearly all of the remaining empire. Cuba became independent, Puerto Rico and

Until recently, Spanish Morocco was a Spanish colony, so that Arab women, like this one, were not an unfamiliar sight in southern Spain.

15.   ARAB WOMAN

23

the Philippines were ceded to the United States. Since 1900, Spain's overseas possessions have diminished almost to the vanishing point. In 1956 Morocco, on the north coast of Africa, the last large area under Spanish control, became an independent state, leaving Spain in control of only scattered outposts consisting of Ifni, an enclave on Morocco's Atlantic coast, Spanish West Africa, with a population of about 200,000, and some small islands off the coast of Africa.

In 1931, the king of Spain abdicated. The Republic, proclaimed that year, soon found that the differences of opinion between political extremes of Right and Left could not be ironed out by debates in parliament. In 1936, the Army, long an active participant in politics, revolted, and a bloody Civil War broke out.

Civil War and Reconstruction

THE CIVIL WAR of 1936–39 brought destruction and suffering to all of Spain. Germany, Italy, and Soviet Russia actively participated in the war, but in the end the party of the Falange, led by Generalissimo Franco, was victorious. Since 1939 Spain has been ruled by the Falange. It is once more a kingdom, though the throne is vacant. In

The Falange is the movement brought into power by its victory in the Spanish Civil War of 1936–39. Its emblem is shown here.

20.   SYMBOL OF THE FALANGE

24

The Valley of the Fallen is a national monument to those who died in the Spanish Civil War. The crypt, carved from sheer rock, is one of the biggest in the world.

World War II Spain remained neutral; since 1954 a treaty linking Spain to the United States allows the construction of American naval and air bases on Spanish soil.

The Spaniard's Home Is His Region

MODERN SPAIN, a land of 195,500 square miles, filling the entire Iberian Peninsula, except for Portugal, stretches from France and the Pyrenees on the north to the Mediterranean Sea on the south and east, and the Atlantic Ocean on the west. It is chiefly a high arid plateau. Though divided into provinces, the old regions, that have been part of Spanish history for centuries, remain the true, meaningful divisions of the country. When a Spaniard is asked about his home, he will proudly state that he is a Gallego, from the northern region of Galicia, a Castellano from the central tableland of Castile, or an Andaluz from the plains of Andalusia in the south, rather than naming the province where he lives. The old rivalries between the regions are not entirely forgotten, though they no longer are argued except in friendly fashion.

Farms and Farmers

O F THE 30 million people of Spain, the vast majority are farmers, and live in villages or small towns. Only two cities have a population of over one million: Madrid, the capital, with about 2 million, and Barcelona, leading seaport on the Mediterranean coast, with about 1.5 million. Spain has considerable unexploited mineral deposits, but industry is handicapped by lack of power and transportation. It is in agriculture, then, that one finds the clue to much of the daily life.

Wheat is by far the leading crop, but yields are low. Recovery from the devastation of the Civil War has been slow for lack of draft animals and fertilizers. Furthermore, only twenty-eight per cent of the farmers

Water is scarce in many parts of Spain. Here a vendor draws water from his barrel as he makes his daily rounds.

The great goatskins shown here take one back to the days of the Bible; in rural Spain, wine is still stored in them, to be drawn off whenever needed.

The Spanish farmer has few tools, fewer machines. Threshing is done the old way, tossing wheat in the air, while the wind carries off the chaff.

work their own land. In the south, a few rich people own enormous sheep ranches. In the irrigated eastern areas, most farms are less than an acre in size and population densities average 500 to the square mile. But the greatest problem confronting the farmer is lack of water, a problem that the government seeks to solve in part by the development of extensive irrigation projects.

Farming in Spain depends on water more than on any other single feature. Most of the country receives little rainfall: on the average, less than twenty inches a year on the central tableland, less than sixteen inches in the east. It is unreliable from year to year, causing sharp fluctuations in yields of wheat, barley, and rye. All too often, crop failures mean buying food from abroad with money that might better be used to import needed farm machinery and fertilizers, to construct new

In the *rias,* the deep, splendid harbors of northwestern Spain, fishermen spread their nets out to dry in the sun.

Markets are centers of city life everywhere in Spain, where people come to do their shopping, in tiny booths on the indoor market, or from street vendors' stalls.

irrigation projects, and to develop industries and better transportation.

It is only in the far north and northwest, in the regions bordering the Atlantic Ocean, that water from the sky, from springs, and from small streams is available all year. Elsewhere water is a precious resource, carefully hoarded in cisterns and reservoirs, truly the base of life over large areas of the countryside.

Northern Spain: Green Country

THE HUMID PARTS of Spain are widely separated, forming a green fringe to a land that is otherwise of red and yellow and gray hues, for man long ago destroyed the natural forest cover. The three historic regions of Galicia, Asturias, and the Basque country in the north, have always lived a little apart from the mainstream of events. A great range

The fountain is always the center of any Spanish village. In this remote place in the northwest, women come to the fountain with their great pitchers, to carry water to their homes.

8.   VILLAGE FOUNTAIN IN GALICIA

of mountains separates much of this region from the heart of Spain, the central tableland. Galicia is the western end of it, where the mountains run out into the sea. The valleys there were invaded by the seas, and each of them forms a magnificent natural harbor, called *ria*. Small towns stand picturesquely on the shores of these harbors, and fishermen put out to sea, looking for sardines, lobster, and herring in the Atlantic.

The Pilgrim's Goal: Santiago

THE MOST IMPORTANT TOWN in Galicia, and in many ways one of the most interesting places in Spain, is Santiago, the shrine of the Apostle St. James. Galicia was one of the few places where Christians found refuge at the time of the Moslem conquest, and this little town where, according to popular belief, St. James was buried, rose to be famous all over Europe. The apostle became the patron saint of Spain, his burial place one of the great pilgrimage centers of Europe, and the name of Santiago Matamoros, St. James the Killer of Moors, the battle cry of Christian Spain in its long wars against the Moslems. The church of the apostle, with its many treasures, remains one of the great shrines of Christendom to this day.

The land of Asturias extends along the northern coast, a narrow band of forest, good pasture, and fertile farms and gardens between the high mountains and the Atlantic. Here are Spain's most important iron and coal mines, and Bilbao and its suburbs, accessible to ocean steamers, bristle with blast furnaces and steel mills, a rare sight of heavy industry in an otherwise rural environment. The beaches along the

The little donkey of this peddler is loaded down with trinkets of earthenware, of straw, of metal. The man demonstrates the use of a small wine bottle.

Atlantic are cool and pleasant when the summer sun is at its hottest in the rest of the peninsula, and men of means patronize them as summer resorts. The seaside towns of Asturias and the neighboring Basque resorts around San Sebastián are among the most beautiful of all Europe.

Ball Games, Berets, and Sheep

THE BASQUE COUNTRY forms part of the borderland of Spain in the north, abutting against the high walls of the Pyrenees. The Basque people are one of the great mysteries of European history. They speak a language not related to any other living tongue, and preserve many of their picturesque customs and quite a few elements of their traditional dress, living as they always have within a small world of their own. Theirs is a land of forests, rich pastures, and good farms in the valleys, of strikingly beautiful beaches along the coast. Their national game, the fast and fascinating *jai alai,* is played not only in Spain but in the Americas as well.

The small "beanie" the Basques like to wear is popular in Spain and in France. The mountains offer excellent summer pasture, and sheep from all over the country used to be herded here during the hot summer months. Basque shepherds and their faithful dogs seem to be just about the world's best, and in recent years hundreds of these mountaineers have been brought to the western United States, where they now herd sheep on the ranges of Nevada and Idaho.

It is through the Basque country that many foreigners, coming from Europe, first enter Spain. Their first impression is an unusual one, underlining at once that this is a country well separated from Europe, to the point of having a system of railroads all its own. All passengers have to change trains at the Spanish-French frontier, for Spanish railroads are broad gauge, the two rails being further apart than on railroads in the rest of Western Europe. The differences between Spain and neighboring France become even stronger when the train suddenly arrives in the wide, open world of the central tableland, the *meseta* of Castile and León.

Land of Castles: Castile

CASTILE AND LEON were the leaders in the fight against the Moslems, and have remained in many respects the leaders of Spain down to our time. The speech of Castile, *lengua castellana,* became the standard of Spanish speech and literature, and a true Castilian always refers to his own mother tongue as *Castellano,* not as *Español.* The name of Castile itself refers to the austere, warlike beginnings of this high, dry, at times hostile country, and to the castles that dot the landscape of the rolling tableland. Except for the central mountains that separate Old Castile, the northern, from New Castile, the southern section, the tableland rolls for 300 miles from the mountains of Asturias to within sight of the plains of Andalusia in the south. There is a monotony about this landscape of short grass and few trees, where villages are hidden in the river valleys that cut down into the land. There is a certain grandeur about it, too, the grandeur of wide, open country, and a range of colors, of red, brown, and yellow, that will remind many an American of Arizona and New Mexico. The Spanish *conquistadores,* men like Coronado and Cabeza de Vaca, who came from Castile and from its western borderland, Estremadura, must have found parts of the American Southwest familiar indeed!

The cities that dot the map of Castile have names that echo down the halls of Spanish history. Burgos, one of Spain's first cities, dominated by the huge mass of its magnificent Gothic Cathedral; Salamanca, once a leader among European universities, where many of the problems of navigation were solved that made the great discoveries possible; León, where tiny churches take the visitor back to the Dark Ages, when the city was a refuge of Christians; above all Toledo, the old

7.   VIEW OF TOLEDO

Toledo, high above the Tajo River, was for centuries Spain's leading city. Though no longer the capital, it is still the seat of the Primate, head of the Spanish Church, and an unsurpassed museum of Spain's past.

33

capital of Spain; these cities of Castile are all landmarks of art, storehouses of beauty, stopping places on any tour of Spain.

Toledo: Museum City of Spain

THREE RIVERS course down the slope of the tableland to the Atlantic. The Duero and the Tajo (or Tagus) run west through Portugal to the Atlantic. The Guadalquivir, that in its lower course becomes the main stream of Andalusia, runs to the south. Toledo stands high above the valley of the Tajo, on a rocky spur surrounded by steep slopes that descend to the river. There the early rulers, Vandal and Goth, had their headquarters, and when the city was retaken from the Moslems, in 1085, it became the capital of the kings of Castile; later, that of the kings of Spain. Within its winding, narrow streets are some of the noblest monuments of the past. The cathedral, in the heart of the city, is a museum itself; each of its chapels represents some phase or other of the long and colorful past of this great church. At one of the altars, Mass according to the Mozarabic rite is still celebrated every day, the rite that Christians living under Moslem rule in old Spain had followed, the rite that was the source of some of the most moving prayers in the Book of Common Prayer of the Church of England.

The making of fine steel objects, ornamented with an intricate pattern of gold inlay, is one of the traditional crafts of Toledo.

13.   TOLEDO ARTISAN AT WORK

The Alcalá Gate in Madrid is one of the capital's most noted landmarks.

Toledo is a true treasure house of art. The house of El Greco stands there just as he left it, and the tiny church around the corner from it proudly displays what many consider his greatest masterpiece, the "Burial of the Count Orgaz." Two of Spain's oldest synagogues, converted into Christian churches, and now open as museums, show unusual blendings of Moslem art with Jewish tradition. And the weary sightseer can always find rest and release from his pilgrimage on the lively square of Zocodover, where he can watch the world go by, sipping his strong coffee, and enjoying the shade beneath awnings that protect him from the midday sun.

"The Desert Begins at the Gates of Madrid"

T OLEDO'S DAYS as the capital of Spain ended when Philip II decided to find a more accessible place whence he could control national

6.   THE ROYAL PALACE, MADRID

The Royal Palace was the residence of the kings of Spain until 1931, the end of the monarchy. Built in the mid-eighteenth century, this great mass of gray granite is one of the main features of Madrid's skyline.

affairs. Madrid, picked by Philip as the new capital, is truly in a central position, being very near the center of the country. Yet as a capital city it suffers from the serious disadvantage of a harsh climate that is given to excesses of heat—midsummer temperatures are often in the nineties and average in the upper eighties—and to cold winds in winter that sweep down from the nearby Sierra. That Madrid has grown through the centuries to become a vast modern city is a tribute to the iron will of kings and chief ministers, for it is still dependent on the far corners of Spain for its daily bread, and the old saying that "the desert begins at the gates of Madrid" is still true.

Modern Madrid is a city of paradoxes. The heart of the city belongs to the twentieth century, with its wide boulevards, handsome business houses, ornate government buildings, and the green oasis of the Retiro

36

gardens. Away from the main thoroughfares Madrid is a city of many small apartments, where life moves at a slow and leisurely pace. This is a country of hot summers and the daily lives of the people include the ritual of the afternoon siesta during the heat of the day. The American visitor is apt to find it difficult at first to adjust himself to the daily schedule. Business and government begin their day late in the forenoon, breaking for lunch around 2 P.M., the lunch being followed by siesta. The most active part of the day is late afternoon and early evening, and most Spaniards have their evening meal between 9 and 10 P.M. Theaters and most other places of amusement follow late schedules, too, but bullfights by tradition are held in the afternoon.

2.

DOWNTOWN MADRID

Madrid is a busy, bustling metropolis. The crossroads shown here are near the heart of the city, where the ancient road to Alcalá meets the Gran Via, where government and private business are conducted.

Madrid, like other major cities, is a place for good food and interesting shops. It is also the nerve center of all activities. Spain has had a strong central government for centuries, and the present regime is no exception. Government controls in business and education are rigid, and all decisions are made in the capital. It is the government, for instance, that is attempting to solve the problems of low industrial production by establishing new factories with public and/or private financing. One of these new factories, a big steel mill near Avilés, wholly owned by the government, was completed and went into operation in 1961. Its capacity of about 750,000 tons almost doubled Spain's production of steel, most of which is exported.

The government has also made serious attempts to improve the operation and equipment of its outmoded railway system. One device instituted is interchangeable axles of freight trains crossing the French-Spanish border to offset the difference in width of track.

Spanish railroads, Spanish highways, Spanish airlines all converge

12.   BULLFIGHT IN MADRID

Bullfights are one of the most popular sports in Spain. Most towns have their own arena, the Plaza de Toros, where the fights are held, attracting huge crowds and providing much color and excitement.

As many as eight people work side by side on the great tapestries, made in the state tapestry works of Madrid. Some of the larger pieces take twelve to eighteen months to complete.

on Madrid, and with the air age the city has also become an important center of air travel between the United States, Western Europe and the Mediterranean world.

And Other Irrigation Projects

To PURCHASE needed cotton, non-ferrous metals, steel products, agricultural machinery, mining equipment, rail and air transportation equipment, Spain sought and obtained foreign aid, much of it from the United States. To improve its position in the European market, in 1959 it became a member of the Organization for European Economic Cooperation; and subsequently instituted a program of economic stabilization, which included the stabilizing of the peseta at 60 to each United States dollar.

Madrid has grown through the centuries to become a vast modern city. Here is a part of the Plaza de España, and a view of the Gran Via with its wide boulevard and handsome business houses.

In 1958, hoping to augment its power resources by the development of oil reserves, a new law was passed permitting foreign companies to explore for oil within Spain and in its African colonies. As a result a number of concessions were given to foreign companies during 1960.

But the most significant economic event of recent years has been an accelerated government program to extend irrigation, reforestation, and the development of hydroelectric power, in some cases as a part of a single large project. Several seasons of acute drought, interspersed with violent and destructive floods, had made the government acutely aware of the joint problems of water and power, and triggered the long-range plans to improve the situation.

Under them several million acres of now dry land will be irrigated, much of it to be devoted to cotton, a valuable export crop. The whole program, only partially completed, involves the building of dozens of dams, some of them among the largest in Europe, the reforestation of eroded hill lands on the watersheds of the lakes created by the dams, and the installation of hydroelectric power facilities in connection with the dams. The various projects are mostly in the northeast and southwest. Among them the largest and most important is the dramatic Badajoz project, in the province of that name in the southwest, where five big dams on the Guadiana River will provide, when completed, an integrated system of water use and land conservation. It will supply water to irrigate more than 300,000 acres and generate a sizable amount of additional electric power, and more than 100,000 acres of eroded hill land will be reforested.

The Avenida José Antonío, known to Madrileños as the Gran Via, is the city's most important thoroughfare, lined with hotels, shops, and cafés.

5. THE GRAN VIA, MADRID

MAP OF
SPAIN
REGIONS and PLACES

1. Galicia   7. Levante
2. Asturia   8. Andalusia
3. Basque   9. Estremadura
4. Navarre   10. New Castile
5. Aragon   11. Old Castile
6. Catalonia   12. Leon

ANDORRA

BARCELONA

MINORCA

MAJORCA

IBIZA

VALENCIA

ELCHE

MURCIA

CARTAGENA

CABO DE GATA

EBRO RIVER

MEDITERRANEAN SEA

Aragón

NORTHEASTERN SPAIN, the valley of the Ebro River, is the region of Aragón. Ferdinand, last king of Aragón, and his wife, Isabella of Castile, were the architects of united Spain and started building its overseas empire. The Ebro River is an opening to the Mediterranean; there is a touch of the south in Aragón: vineyards on the hillsides, irrigated fields and gardens along the riverbanks. Away from the Ebro to the north the land rises swiftly, toward the heights of the Pyrenees.

Over 300 miles long, the Pyrenees are the mountain wall that separates Spain from the rest of Europe. In their high valleys sheep find summer pasture. Great reservoirs have been constructed there to produce hydroelectric power, to supplant Spain's meager resources of fuel. There is a lonely grandeur about the Pyrenean peaks; it takes an eagle or an experienced mountaineer to find the way among the crags from the Spanish to the French side. Four railroads cross the Pyrenees today, and though Spanish speech has spread to some extent across the mountains to France, the crests that tower between the two countries represent the oldest and the most stable frontier in all Europe.

Lamb is a favorite with Spaniards, especially at Christmas and Easter. A butcher inspects carcasses just brought in from the countryside.

El Pueblo Español, Barcelona. The "Spanish Village," built for the International Fair of 1929, contains reproductions of some famous buildings and various types of architecture found in Spain, as well as workshops demonstrating the best-known Spanish crafts.

Catalonia by the Sea

THE EASTERN END of the Pyrenees, their foothills, and the narrow coastal lowland along the Mediterranean together form one of the country's smallest yet most individual regions, Catalonia. The people of Catalonia were among the first to obtain their independence from the Moslems, and around the Catalonian capital of Barcelona a strong state was formed that led in the commerce of the Mediterranean for centuries. It was in Catalonia and in the neighboring Balearic Islands that the art of making maps for the seaman was first developed in Europe, an indispensable skill for long sea voyages.

The long tradition of Catalonian independence made the speech of Catalonia different from that of Castile, and though the little country was soon swallowed up by its powerful neighbors, to become part of the united Spanish kingdom, the tradition of independence was never quite lost. Nowadays it is evident in the survival of Catalonian literature, quite separate from Spanish, and in times of free political discus-

45

sions the Catalonian always follows his own bent and is given to political extremes.

Among the towns of Catalonia Barcelona has always outshone all others. It is the leading seaport of Spain, an important trading center, and the heart of the nation's greatest industrial area. The suburbs of Barcelona and the city itself are known for their metalworks, textile mills, leather factories, chemical plants, and for the small factories making cork products, for Barcelona lies within a short distance of the true Mediterranean part of the country, the East, or Levante, where cork oak is one of the principal trees.

Levante: Olives and Oranges

SOUTH OF BARCELONA the long, low eastern coast stretches into the distance. This is a land of long summer droughts, where the earth becomes so dry that deep cracks appear, a land where the short season of winter rains cannot support farming, or even vegetation except for dry stubble and cacti. Here the art of irrigation, introduced during the centuries of Moslem rule, wrought miracles and established a row of oases, vivid spots of verdure in a harsh and arid land.

The towns on this coast are surrounded by gardens, or *huertas.* Water is a precious, carefully husbanded resource; every tiny stream is controlled by wicker weirs and tiny walls, every farmer is entitled to a share of the water to irrigate his land. Out in these *huertas* the houses,

46

The statue of Columbus, Admiral of the Ocean Sea, surveys the great harbor of Barcelona, Spain's busiest port.

The monastery of Montserrat nestles against a mountain-side near Barcelona. There has been a Benedictine mon-astery here for over 1,200 years, a favorite goal of pilgrims, one of the ancient sanctuaries of Spain.

47

built of adobe with thatched roofs and whitewashed walls, are hidden among orchards and olive groves. Oranges and lemons, almonds, peaches, grapes, great fields of onions, lettuce, and beans are grown and irrigation rights are the farmers' most valued possession.

Tribunals, formed by the farmers, decide on all cases where the right to use water is questioned; their decision, based on unwritten laws handed down from Moslem days of over a thousand years ago, is final, and accepted by all. In the city of Valencia the water tribunal meets every Thursday in the shadow of the Gate of the Apostles, the great

Spain is one of the world's great producers of olives; olive oil generally replaces butter and fat in Spanish cooking.

18.   IN A SPANISH OLIVE GROVE

gate of the cathedral. There the tribunal hears the complainants and passes judgment. Water has formed here a tightly knit, closely organized society, whose very existence depends on its wise and just decisions.

The contrast between dry and irrigated land is striking everywhere along this coast line. Outside of the *huertas* the land appears abandoned. Only small watchtowers dot the coast, where constant vigil used to be kept, to warn people of the approach of Moslem raiders from Africa. In the foothills inland there are mines of lead, silver, and copper, exploited since the days of Rome, and still producing small amounts of metal which is shipped away for smelting and refining.

Africa in Spain: an Oasis Town

THE EASTERN COAST of Spain is within an easy day's sail of North Africa. The desert is just over the horizon, and in one place at least its breath is clearly felt, in the great palm groves of Elche. Elche is a small town, a few miles from the coast, and it is set in the midst of a vast forest of date palms, like an oasis amidst the desert. It is a place inhabited since before the beginnings of recorded history, and the strange and beautiful statue of a woman found here, known as the Lady of Elche, is one of the earliest remains of civilization on Spanish soil.

In the south of Spain even wintry days afford people a chance to be outdoors. Here Sevillanos enjoy the warm sun, protected by high buildings on the old exhibition grounds of the city.

4. RELAXING IN THE SUN, SEVILLE

49

Streets in most Spanish towns are narrow, covered with cobble-
stones. People spend a great deal of time on the street, and much
business is conducted in cafés and on street corners.

The towns of the east are seaports, like Valencia and Cartagena, or
inland centers, a short distance from the sea, like Murcia. The vineyards make a strong, heady wine, the fields produce wheat, the olive
groves provide olive oil. There are fishing smacks putting out to sea
every day, for fish is an important food in Spain. The range of colors
is striking, the brilliant white of houses, the emerald green of grains in
the spring, the soft, gray-green of the olive tree, the brilliant tints of
blossoming fruit trees.

Islands of Paradise

ALL THE FEATURES of the Spanish Mediterranean coast appear in an almost exaggerated way in the Balearic Islands that lie less than a hundred miles away. The three principal islands, Mallorca, Menorca, and Ibiza, have escaped many of the problems that confront the rest of the country. Life in these islands is simple, moving at a very slow pace; they are indeed an ideal retreat from the pressures of modern living. As year-round resorts, they are unsurpassed in the charm of their setting, the calm of their existence, and last but not least, low expenses, though their increasing popularity as an international playground tends to make costs higher each year.

The Canary Islands, just off the coast of northwestern Africa, south of Spain, were one of its first overseas possessions (1496). They consist of seven major islands with a total land area of 2800 square miles,

The Church of La Concepción in La Laguna, Canary Islands, contains the Cross of the Conquest and British flags captured from Admiral Nelson.

and a population of some 680,000. But only two are really inhabited, Las Palmas and Tenerife, each with about half the group's population. Of volcanic origin, the islands are rugged, with peaks rising to 12,000 feet. They are richly verdant, gay with flowers, and have a mild, pleasant climate which is attracting an increasing number of European vacationers. Though they once produced good wine, the leading crops are now sugar cane, tomatoes, and bananas. The two biggest towns, Las Palmas and Santa Cruz, are important fueling ports.

The Rock: Gibraltar

NEAR CABO DE GATA, the Cape of the Cat, the Spanish coast turns sharply to the west, and the high ramparts of the Sierra Nevada

A tobacco drying hut in La Orotava, Canary Islands.

Las Palmas on Grand Canary Island has become a famed tourist resort, particularly in winter. This gay city features palm-lined beaches and luxuriant parks, and you can even visit the house where Columbus stopped on his first voyage. Las Palmas was founded in 1478.

appear above the coast line, seemingly a short distance away. Andalusia begins there, where Moslem rule lasted until the thirteenth century, a land different in many ways from the rest of the country. The southern coast of Andalusia, as far as the Strait of Gibraltar, is a narrow line between the blue waters of the Mediterranean and the yellow, parched heights of the Sierra. Tiny towns hug the shore line, surrounded by vineyards famous for their grapes and their wine. Málaga, the principal town, is as famous for its raisins in Europe as Fresno is in the United States.

Gibraltar, the Rock, as it is known throughout the British Commonwealth, stands guard over the strait, one of the great seaways of the world. The men of antiquity called the strait the Pillars of Hercules, believing that the ocean beyond was an evil place, haunted by spirits. The Phoenicians were especially wont to support this tale, for it gave them a free hand to trade beyond Gibraltar with the copper miners of western Spain and the tin miners of England. Gibraltar, then, has been

53

The ruins of an eleventh-century castle of the
Knights Templars still stand in Torija, Guadalajara.

a prize to mariners for over 3,000 years, and England, having conquered it in 1704, has relished its possession ever since. During World
War II Gibraltar was one of the vital Allied bases for sea and air opera-
tions.

Land of the West: El Andalus

ANDALUSIA was the Land of the West to Islam, the westernmost
territory they had conquered and held for any length of time.
The five centuries of their rule left a lasting mark on the land, its people, its language, its buildings, even on the names of cities, rivers, and
mountains.

Andalusia is a hot and dry land, dependent upon the waters of the
river Guadalquivir for its existence. Wandering about Andalusia one

This narrow, cobblestone street winds through the little
Spanish town of Sigüenza, on the banks of the Henares River.

cannot help but feel that there is a great charm about the countryside: tiny white donkeys trotting along the highway, carrying great sacks of grain to a mill, a piece of Moorish architecture, a mill driven by the waters of a small, swift stream, fields of wheat, orchards, vineyards, and orange groves stretching to the horizon. The horizon itself is always dominated by uplands, the high ranges of the Sierra Nevada in the east, the dry, desolate heights of the Sierra Morena in the north.

To the north of Andalusia, amidst the Sierra Morena whose barren flanks cover the land like the waves of a frozen sea, are some of Spain's most valuable resources: the copper mines of Río Tinto, and the mer-

cury mines of Almadén, the world's greatest. These are mines that have operated since before the time of Christ, and their surroundings, with enormous tailings of debris, look like the mountains of the moon.

Seville, on the Guadalquivir River, is Andalusia's first city, and one of the handsomest in all Spain. The imprint of centuries of Islam is strong throughout Seville, in the marvels of stonework that decorate the Alcázar Palace, in the gardens and fountains, in the great tower of the Giralda that stands above the city. The cathedral is justly considered one of the most beautiful in Europe. But Seville is also known for its roses that bloom all year, for its Spring Fair, and for its religious processions where all the pomp of the Church is displayed.

Segovia is one of the museum towns of Spain. At the top of the rocky spur where the town stands, the Alcázar, once a royal castle, dominates the scene.

Gypsy Music at Its Best

SEVILLE and the land of Andalusia have long been famous as the home of the *gitanos*, the gypsies of Spain, and as the source of much that is best in Spanish folk music. The gypsy dances, like the vivid and vigorous flamenco dance, and gypsy tunes of Andalusia have indeed been the source of inspiration for many composers. There is a haunting quality in many folk songs, sung to the accompaniment of a guitar in Andalusia, and the quick and strong gypsy dances are the best known of Spanish folk dances.

In the fall, when grapes are ripe, they are harvested in great woven baskets. Spain's beasts of burden, donkeys, carry the baskets to the wine presses.

In some of the small towns of southern Spain, streets are so narrow mirrors have been set up on the corners to show whether any traffic is coming from the side streets. This one is in San Fernando, near Cádiz.

Street scene in Seville. This colorful city has frequently been depicted in literature and music. Among the most notable examples are "Carmen," "Don Juan," and "The Barber of Seville."

Cádiz is called *La Tacita de Plata,* or Silver Platter because of its scrupulously clean streets and whitewashed buildings. This is the garden and façade of the Church, Nuestra Senora del Carmen.

Located on a point of land, Cádiz is accessible to the visitor only through this medieval fortified gate.

Sherry at Jérez

SOUTH OF SEVILLE lies the district of Jérez. The golden grapes of Jérez, carefully picked and pressed, yield juice that is judiciously aged and blended, to make sherry, the wine that was so dear to Shakespeare. Cádiz, in white splendor astride its harbor, the best in southern Spain, now serves as the ocean port of Andalusia, Seville being too shallow for the great ships.

Spain is many things to many men. To the student, it presents an unbroken record of history longer than that of most European nations. To the artist and the art collector, it is a land where old stone and old bricks, fine buildings and great paintings, magnificent cathedrals and simple peasant homes form an incomparable background, an inexhaustible happy hunting ground. To the traveler, it offers the great reward of a country where life proceeds at a slow, leisurely pace, where many of the social graces are still very much observed, a country where high-

22.   SPRING FAIR, SEVILLE

On holidays people like to don festive garb and parade on foot or on horseback in the streets of the Spanish towns.

ways and byways are a continuously changing kaleidoscope of varied climates and people, an adventure in the search for beauty. The glory that was Spain in the days of its world empire is past, but it lives on in the stones of the cities, in the dignity of its citizens, in the charm of their old-fashioned courtesy.

Far in the south lie the sunny vineyards of Jérez de la Frontera, home of Spain's most famous wine, sherry.

24.   GRAPE HARVEST, SOUTHERN SPAIN

17.   THE WALLS OF AVILA

The massive walls of Avila, a small and picturesque town north of Madrid, were built in 1090–99, and are still in perfect condition. Measuring over a mile, they entirely surround the town.

USEFUL INFORMATION ABOUT SPAIN

Travel Documents

If you are a United States citizen you need a valid passport but not a visa; nor do you need a certificate or evidence of health. If you plan to remain in Spain six months or more you will need a residence permit obtained from the Direccion General de Seguridad in Madrid, or the civil government in the provinces.

Currency

Spain has a free money market, in which the legal rate of exchange for the peseta, official unit of currency, is 60 to the U.S. dollar. There are 100 centimos in a peseta. You can take in to the country 10,000 pesetas ($166.66), but it is illegal to take out more than 2,000 pesetas. Nor can you take out of the country a larger sum than you took in.

Import Duties and Quotas

You can take in to Spain personal effects without paying duty, which includes a reasonable amount of tobacco.

Some Important Dates in Spanish History

B.C.
201   Spain becomes a Roman province (Hispania).

A.D.
409   Vandal conquest of Spain.
466–711   Visigothic rule over Spain.
711–715   Moslem conquest of Spain.
800–900   Rise of Christian kingdoms in northern Spain.
1085   Toledo recaptured by Christians.
1212   Victory of Las Navas de Tolosa, Moslems restricted to southern-most Spain.

1479   Marriage of Ferdinand of Aragón and Isabella of Castile, the "Catholic Kings."

1492   Fall of Granada, end of Moslem rule in Spain; Columbus discovers America.

1516–1556   Charles I, of Hapsburg, ruler of Spain.

1556–1598   Philip II.

1588   Defeat of the Spanish Armada by the English.

1808–1814   Peninsular War: Spain and England against Napoleon.

1873–1874   First Spanish Republic.

1931–1936   Second Spanish Republic.

1936–1939   Spanish Civil War.

1936–   General Franco, Chief of the Spanish State.

1955–   Spain admitted to the United Nations.

1956–   Spanish Morocco, largest Spanish-controlled area outside Spain, becomes an independent nation.

1958–   Spain joins International Monetary Fund.

1959–   Comprehensive program of economic stabilization instituted; Spain becomes member of Organization for European Economic Cooperation. (OEEC).

Handy Words and Phrases in Spanish

English	Spanish
Good morning or good day	Buenas días
Good afternoon	Buenas tardes
Good evening or good night	Buenas noches
Good-by	Adiós
How are you?	¿Cómo está usted?
How do you say in Spanish?	¿Cómo se dice en Español?
Fine	Perfectamente
Very good	Muy bien, Muy bueno
It's all right	Está bien
Good luck	Buena suerte
Hello	Hola (pronounced "ola")
Come back soon	Vuelva pronto

Where is the hotel?	¿Donde está el hotel?
How much does this cost?	¿Cuante cuesta esto?
How do you feel?	¿Cómo se siente usted?
How goes it?	¿Qué tal?
Pleased to meet you	Mucho gusto en conocerle
The pleasure is mine	El gusto es mío
I have the pleasure of introducing Mr. . . .	Tengo el gusto de presentarle al Señor . . .
I like it very much	Me gusto mucho
I don't like it	No me gusto
Many thanks	Muchas gracias
Don't mention it	De nada
Pardon me	Perdone usted, Perdóneme
Are you ready?	¿Esta listo?
I am ready	Estoy listo
Welcome	Bienvenida
I am very sorry	Lo siento mucho
What time is it?	¿Qué hora es?
I am glad to see you	Mucho gusto en verle
I understand	Comprendo
Whenever you please	Cuando guste
Please wait	Espere, por favor
I will be a little late	Llegaré un poco tarde

✐✐✐✐ ABOUT THE AUTHOR ✐✐✐✐

GEORGE KISH, a native of Hungary, received his education in Europe and did postgraduate work at the University of Michigan, where he is Associate Professor of Geography. He has traveled through most of Europe, as well as in the United States and Canada, and has been publishing books and articles on geography since 1935.